Cicero, the great Roman rhetorician, taught that an orator or writer has three primary duties: to teach, to delight, and to move. In this book, Mary Anne [M.A.K.] successfully does all three.

Pain and loss come to all of us! The Bible says they are as sure as the sparks fly upward. Pain and loss come in many forms and levels of intensity. The question is not "will they come?" but "what will we do *when* they come?" And will the anchor of our lives be sufficient to keep us from shipwreck when the waves of adversity start lashing against the walls of our world? Mary Anne regularly discovers the antidote in the still, small Voice of God whispering words of comfort, reassurance, and promise.

God Lives in Detroit and Vacations in Other Places is a manual for weary warriors! Through its riveting pages we are led step by step as empathetic observers of Mary Anne's pain and loss, to a clearer understanding that self-awareness, combined with self-acceptance, form the breeding ground to a fuller, more purposeful and fulfilling life. Truly, when the student is ready, the lesson is there.

This book will better equip you to be the "comfort" God designed for you to be to other struggling sojourners just passing through (2 Corinthians 1:4).

Through straight talk, humour, and an amazing dose of personal transparency, Mary Anne teaches us not to waste our sorrows and makes the point that God's address has not changed! He waits to hear from you.

A genuinely engaging and uplifting book full of hard-won insight. Enjoy!

Well done!

—Pastor Glen R. Pitts
Former National Director
Canadian Bible Society,
Director Cities of the World/Campus
Crusade for Christ,
and Vice-President Tyndale Foundation

GOD
Lives in
Detroit

(AND VACATIONS IN OTHER PLACES)

M.A.K. Moran

GOD LIVES IN DETROIT AND VACATIONS IN OTHER PLACES
Copyright © 2016 by M.A.K. Moran

Dream House photo courtesy of Lisa Luevanos of Detroit, Michigan.
lisaluevanos.com. Used by permission.
Photo of shell of business by Ted Lacki

ISBN: 978-1-4866-1245-1   Printed in Canada

Word Alive Press
131 Cordite Road, Winnipeg, MB R3W 1S1
www.wordalivepress.ca

Cataloguing in Publication may be obtained through Library and Archives Canada

I dedicate this book to:

*My God, for never leaving me, or forsaking me,
even when I couldn't remember His address
and
Detroit, the city that never stopped loving me.*

Contents

Acknowledgements

How is it possible to give adequate thanks to God? He knew the true desires of my heart and waited for me with a love so perfect it healed a place in me that I thought would forever be torn open, jagged, and ripped beyond repair. I am in awe of Your goodness and mercy. I am forever thankful.

To my precious children, you have born the toughest part of my journey. When I was a mere shell of what I once had been, you held steadfast in your love. You are, and have always been, the most purposeful part of my life. I thank God for you and for all He has taught me through you. My love for you will endure forever. *I Love You ... a bushel and a peck!*

To my grandchildren, my Darlings, there were times you were the reason I felt my life would go on. Your innocent and unencumbered love for me was, at times, the only factor that held the pieces of my heart together. I am most thankful for the moments when

God spoke to me through you. You hold a place in my heart reserved for no other. I will love you without limit all the days of my life.

To my Detroit Lovelies, my lifelong friends (no matter where you live now), you have loved me like no other friends are capable of, and you make me laugh until it hurts. Our hearts are linked through an invisible, unbreakable chain of love, laughter, and a continued support for each other—not to mention Mexican food and the world's greatest music. I thank God I grew up in the best of times, with the best of friends, in a city whose "best" will always remain in my heart.

To Faye Mathie, I surely would not have survived the last four years without you. The gifts God has instilled in you as a counselor are literally a life-giving treasure. If there is a silver lining in my grief, it is that what started as a client relationship has now bloomed into a beautiful friendship. You truly are God with skin on to me. I look forward to years of fun times and adventures with you. I would be remiss in not thanking your husband, Stewart, for being willing to carry all my "stuff" when we are all together on a shopping spree. He's a keeper!

To my Church Family and my faith-filled friends, it is an enormous comfort for me to know that in my darkest hours there are those of you that have stood, and still stand, in the gap for me. You are not merely my friends but also a powerful army that can call on the forces of Heaven on my behalf when I simply have no strength to do so myself. You are the faithful. I thank God for you.

Foreword

Romans 15:13, ESV: *May the God of hope fill you with all joy and peace in believing, so that by the power of the Holy Spirit you may abound in hope.*

Every once in a while in a lifetime, someone comes into your life and your surroundings, and you immediately stop, stand up tall, and take notice.

M.A.K. (Mary Anne) is that someone to the hundreds (thousands) of people who have been blessed to know her and refer to her as friend!

A woman of God. Refined by God. Sent by God. Used by God.

As you read through the pages of this book, you will quickly begin to see how easy it was for me to write this.

M.A.K. takes us on a journey—her journey. One not travelled easily.

As her story unfolds, you will feel the impact of a life that, from its commencement, was marred by the sins and abuse of others, during a time that should only be filled with innocence and laughter.

That was only the beginning.

The many continuing chapters of her life would come to be filled with deep holes to climb out of, and dark dungeons where there seemed to be no light.

Somehow, through grace and plans designed by an awesome God, throughout M.A.K.'s life, His light removed the darkness that at times sought to cripple her... and she was rescued.

With God's never-ending help, she kept climbing out from under the shadow, the loneliness, the seemingly hopeless life events.

By the time you read the last phrase—"for the One"—you will realize that the diamond in the rough has been refined, and today stands, shining as only one of God's prized jewels is able.

This story will restore your faith in a living, loving, Heavenly Father, and will challenge you in a fresh way to once again give God your address.

Your hope will be restored, you will find yourself dreaming again, and you will sense a desire to live like never before!

—Pastor Craig Head
Executive Pastor
Mapleview Community Church

Preface

There are times and circumstances that generate a pain so deep that even the most seasoned believer can feel separated from God. A pit so consuming and dark that the thought of finding Him again, and feeling His touch, seems impossible.

I know that place… the forsaken zone. The place where time stands still and the plan for our lives seems muffled and nearly wiped out. In that despair, God gave me His address, so I would be able to come to the place where He lives and open the door to His heart… and my future.

During this journey, I realized that mere faith is not enough to sustain me. Only when our faith is combined with a willingness to surrender to His plan can power and strength rise within our souls.

God never condemned me when I did not immediately run to Him, arms wide open with strength and vigour to complete the race that was set before me.

When I was crawling through the mud, barely able to drag myself through, He knelt at the finish line. He did not tower above me; He went below the crowd, below the noise, so that when I looked up long enough to take a breath, I would be able to see Him waving me on to the finish line.

I sincerely hope that as the words on the pages of this book enter your mind, in your heart you will realize that there has never been a moment in your life when He hasn't been there, waiting for you where He lives. Just look for His address... it's in the book.

chapter one
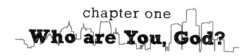 Who are You, God?

Who is God? How many times do you think this short three-word question has been asked? (Not to mention how many diverse brilliant philosophical, scientific, and theological minds have pondered, researched, and documented the answer.)

I am certainly no genius, and my philosophical and theological thoughts and expertise are somewhat limited. I can, however, tell you with utmost confidence that I know, experientially, that there *is a God.*

I have felt Him in ways that literally took my breath away. He has spoken to me in a still small voice and through magnanimous life experience encounters that proclaimed His words at a near deafening level.

We Complicate God

Personally, I think we complicate God far more than we need to. In chapter 3 of the book of Exodus, God tells us who He is. In verse 13, Moses asks, *"When I go to the Israelites and say to them, 'The God of your ancestors sent me to you,' they will ask me, 'What is his name?' So what can I tell them?"* In Verse 14*: "God said, 'I am who I am.'"*[1] It is also sometimes translated, *"I will be what I will be."*

> "God said, 'I am who I am.'" It is also sometimes translated, "I will be what I will be."

You may be thinking, "Okay? So what exactly does that mean? What kind of name is that?" I can only tell you what it means to me.

We tend to identify each other by our names. Those who know me personally have certain feelings that arise when they hear "Mary Anne O'Reilly." Those are feelings of younger-year adventures, friendships and experiences while I was growing up, before I was married. Those who hear the name

---

1 GNT.

"Mary Anne Moran" think of the years I spent as a wife, mother, grandmother, professional, and currently, the author of this book. The fact remains that each scenario or experience my name evokes is limited by time, environment, and circumstance.

The predicament that comes about when attempting to categorize God by His name is that He cannot be named. He is ineffable, He is incomprehensible, and He is not limited by time, environment or circumstances, only by the confines of our human minds. He is limitless. When speaking to Him, I call Him God, Father, Saviour, Almighty. However, when I experience or feel Him, He is truly the great I Am.

If you are having difficulty grasping this, do you remember the moment you first felt an emotion so intense it took your breath away? You were moved to tears because you had no words … because there were no words. That barely comes close to the experience of being connected to God, understanding He is simply *there*, at all times and in all things.

That Still Small Voice

Even though I remember the moment I first experienced hearing that "still small voice" in my head (that

I know now was God), I don't remember the first time I knew He was *there*. Even at a very young age, I had a unique understanding that I was being led by something greater than myself. That "something powerful" was actually grieving with me in my pain while continuing to cradle and strengthen me.

> I remember the moment I first experienced hearing that "still small voice" in my head (that I know now was God).

It was around the age of four that I realized other people had a name for Him. It was God—although, as I grew I often thought they shortchanged who He was. I wondered if they knew that, in the midst of pain or evil, it was God that held you up and pulled you through. Did they understand He was the greatest force of love and goodness ever known or felt? Did they know He was and is the *I Am*?

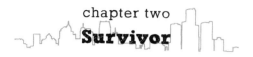

chapter two

*"To continue to exist or live after ...
to function"*[2]

If there was anything my life's circumstances had indoctrinated into the core of my being, it was the knowledge that I was, indeed, able to *endure*. It would become a strength that took root deep within my soul at a very early age.

My furthest memories stem back to probably the age of three or four. Even then, with limited capability to reason or understand life's complexities, I felt different. It's hard to explain, actually, but I sensed an inner stamina that swirled inside my mind

---

2 *Merriam Webster's Dictionary and Thesaurus*, s.v. "Survivor." Springfield, MA: Encyclopedia Britannica Co., 2007. Also available at http://www.merriam-webster.com.

> I sensed an inner stamina that swirled inside my mind amidst a life of chaos, insecurity, and pain. I was a survivor!

amidst a life of chaos, insecurity, and pain. I was a survivor!

My childhood was less than picturesque. By the time I was born, my parents' marriage was in a state of continual turmoil and toxicity. As I grew up, I saw and heard things children shouldn't. Instead of glee-filled childhood wonder, I frequently felt abandoned and afraid.

Life's "Unanswerables"

I knew without a doubt that my father loved me. He never failed to demonstrate that; however, his alcoholism hindered any form of security from being present in our home. It was difficult for me to understand how my prince charming, the man who danced with me as I stood on his shoes, tucked me into bed singing *I love you, a bushel and a peck,* and spoke kindness and wisdom into my life on our Daddy-and-his-little-girl walks together, could transform into a hate-filled man who would fight venomously with my mother at a moment's notice.

It was equally as difficult and distressing to comprehend what I could have done as a child that caused my mother to be frequently distanced from me yet cling to my sister as if she were a prized jewel. I thought my mother was the most beautiful woman that ever lived; however, not even her beauty was capable of disguising the ugly dysfunction within the relationship she shared with my father. It was not until much later in life that I understood the level of her own personal pain and the family dynamic that divided us.

But… I survived.

At a very young and unprotected age, I became the victim of an evil depravity that drove my grandfather to prey on me to satisfy a sick uncontrollable want to sexually molest me. The depth of that perverted desire culminated in an act of mental suffering and physical injury no child should have to endure.

But … I survived.

I grew in years, stamina, and the desire to escape my life for something better. I did just that. I married young into the perfect family to start my perfect new life. And yet, it wasn't perfect. It wasn't long before I felt the sting of the same isolation I had endured in my childhood, accompanied by venomous degradation, betrayal, and a gradual withering away of my confidence and self-worth.

I suffered many miscarriages during those times, and even though I was told to resign myself to the fact I might never give birth to a child of my own, at the age of twenty-three I was finally blessed with a beautiful miracle: my baby girl.

The moment of that joy was short lived, however, when in my hospital room on the following day I came face to face with the reality of meeting my husband's mistress.

My marriage failed.

But … I survived.

Survival 101

I survived because I knew where to find God. I knew He was on my side. At times I felt I could hear Him cry with me. Thankfully, very early on, I obtained a certain and undeniable knowledge of the fact that I was living in a world that was not evolving in any manner according to the original plan God had begun at creation. This pain wasn't at all what He had planned for my life. I understood God had given mankind free will, and with that came not only the power to do good but also the capability to destroy someone's spirit and drive while seeking the fulfillment of selfish desires and control. God was seeing me *through* to what would one day end and release me to the exact place He desired me to be—with Him.

The side altar at St. Andrews.

I recall kneeling at the side altar of St. Andrews Church when I was feeling afraid and weak in spirit after many attempts to fight off my grandfather and his predatory practices. I begged God for a miracle.

In school we had been learning about Bernadette Soubirous, the fourteen-year-old girl who witnessed the first in a series of apparitions at Lourdes. Kneeling there, I asked for one of the statues to manifest a sign in my presence, as possibly that would deem me to be someone special, chosen by God. Surely then my mother would love me and my grandfather would be afraid to touch me.

I waited and waited, but nothing. The statue remained the same. I begged and cried for what seemed an eternity, and then it happened. I heard that still small voice for the very first time. It was a voice I would grow to know–not an audible voice but words from God that flooded my spirit.

A warm calmness came over me, and in that moment God spoke. *You already have the miracle, Mary Anne. The miracle is that you belong to Me.*

I had no idea what those words meant, but they calmed me and God's presence filled me. Those were the words I clung to for years to come. They were my weapon of survival.

> God spoke. You already have the miracle, Mary Anne. The miracle is that you belong to Me.

And survive I did! And it was worth it!

In 1982, through some very unusual circumstances, I met a man who would change my life forever. He was everything I had ever hoped and prayed for. It wasn't just that he was incredibly handsome, he was perfect for me. God knew what I needed. From the moment we met,

I knew Michael thought I was the most spectacular woman who ever lived. He made that evident in every word he spoke and every action that pertained to me.

When we first began dating, I was often taken off guard when I would look up to find him staring at me. He later told me it was not only because he thought I was beautiful, but it was as if he could see into my heart and soul and the beauty there took his breath away. It didn't take long for me to fall head over heels in love with him.

The Note

I was cautious in the beginning. I had grown not to trust men, and I would not allow myself to be hurt again. We had dated for some time before a particular evening when I was at his home for dinner and a movie (he cooked, big bonus!). That night he reminded me that, one month before, I had commented about a note he had written and put into his wallet. At the time he had said it was just something he needed to remind himself of at a later date.

With a very serious look on his face, he removed his wallet from his back pocket, retrieved the note and handed it to me. It was dated a month earlier, and on it were written these words: *She is the most precious woman on earth, world's greatest kisser, and I know I love her. If in one month I take this note and hand it to her, I know God has put us together.* I bawled like a baby that hadn't been fed in a week.

That evening during the movie Michael fell asleep with his head on my lap. I stroked his beautiful wavy hair and looked at his strong hand holding mine. I wondered if he really knew what he was in for.

I didn't trust men, any men. No man had ever totally protected me from harm or evil. Although he treated me like a princess on her way to being crowned queen, I came with multiple levels of insecurity. It would be awhile before I could let my guard down, if ever. I was at a place in my life when I wasn't sure I even loved myself, so how would I love him enough?

> No man had ever totally protected me from harm or evil.

It was evident that Michael had a deep belief in God, and I was very grateful we shared a common faith. But would it be strong enough for us to weather what would lie before us?

My biggest concern was, of course, my daughter, Angela. I would have died before making a commitment that would harm her in any way. I had gone through hell to become her mother and she was a gift from God to me. I took that more seriously than anything else on earth. Michael would have to love her with all the care, concern, and faithfulness he had shown toward me to that point.

The other major factor was that Michael had full custody of his two daughters. Tracy was three years older than Angela, and Courtney, eight months younger. And they were all so very young. I had grown to love them, and the thought of having two more children in my life when I was certain I would never give birth again seemed like an answered prayer. But I feared not being all they might need. As with Angela, I was not willing to subject them to any further pain in their lives if they couldn't adapt to me. I had no idea how to blend a family.

I stared at Michael for the longest time, and when he gradually opened his eyes, he gave me a wink and asked, "So, where do we go from here?"

Jokingly, I said, "Put the note back in your wallet and ask me in another month."

I knew then that Michael understood exactly what he was in for. He had already committed himself to me and all he knew I could be and to the role he would play in bringing that to fruition.

We married on May 31, 1985.

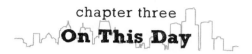

chapter three
On This Day

I could hardly believe the level of emotion and degree of love I was feeling as I stood across from the man I knew loved me more than life, listening to him proclaim a covenant to me before God that was never to be broken. I watched a tear fall down his cheek as he stated, "On this day, I marry my best friend, the woman I laugh with, live for, and love with all my being." Those were not idle words for the benefit of the guests; they were a declaration of how he felt and how he planned to live.

Live that way, we did. He was my best friend, and rarely would a day go by that we didn't laugh until we nearly cried. I often told him I questioned his sanity by sheer virtue of what he could find humour in.

Michael and I on our wedding day.

The Locked Door

I knew Michael understood me to the fullest and was committed to loving and nurturing me to the point of knowing and pursuing my full potential. The penalty I paid for the suffering I had previously endured in my life was a locked door to the greatness of my gifts, talents, and capabilities. He saw those gifts in me long before I did. He removed the lock and opened the door slowly.

Michael encouraged me and I began to bloom. With the growth and change came levels of discomfort and a few good fights along the way. He had a very special way of saying my name when I was wrong that always made me smile and turn around. However, he demanded that I stand up for myself—oppose him if I felt I needed to—without any fear of him leaving or forsaking me. That was the hardest reality for me to grasp hold of, but I knew he was my safety net for any mistake I would make.

He had also been through a failed marriage, and he purposed ours would be the best ever seen. I would sometimes tease him about how he looked at our marriage like it was a business with enormous benefits. We attended any marriage enrichment class we thought would make us a better couple. Living in a house with four women, Michael read everything he could get his hands on about the way women feel and react.

One time in particular, after he had just finished reading a book, I experienced a very difficult day in meetings with a company that had contracted my work and was blabbing away about it. A few minutes into it, I stopped and looked at him in surprise that he hadn't commented. With a look of questioning and shock, he said, "Aren't I just supposed to listen and not fix anything? That's what the book said!" I laughed and couldn't have hugged him tighter.

Except for his relationship with God, nothing came before me.

My greatest gift, without any doubt, was the *way* he loved me. He began every day praying for me. He kept a notebook of my struggles and anything I was working towards, so he was able to be specific in his prayers.

> My greatest gift, without any doubt, was the way he loved me.

He loved and respected me as though I were the most important person on earth, and he never failed to let me know how he hated to be away from me. In fact, early on in our relationship we were on the phone when he said he just never wanted to be the one to say goodbye. So, we began a practice of saying, "I love you," and then starting a countdown, "1... 2..." and on "3" we would hang up so neither of us had to be the one to say it.

We raised our family and made plans for our future. I gained strength and experience, and eventually I became the professional Michael always knew was in me. He encouraged even the craziest parts of my personality.

He was my cheerleader extraordinaire. Many times I would lie next to him in bed while he held me tight and positioned his hand so my face would be cradled in it. He would whisper, "There is no place you will ever be safer." He was right.

A Perpetual Honeymoon

Our children grew and married, and finding ourselves as empty nesters was like being on a perpetual honeymoon. I remember him getting ready to go to work on the last day before his retirement. For more than two decades I had made his lunch and put a note in it. When I saw him standing there, so handsome in his uniform, I began to cry. He was confused because we had been so looking forward to it. I blurted out, "no more notes."

He took my face in his hands and very seriously said, "For all these years you have supported me as a policeman's wife in every manner imaginable—the stress, the worry, and especially the unknown—and never once have you complained. It's my turn to support you. I'll write the notes from now on."

He was in seventh heaven when he retired. He would wake up each morning, kiss me, and say, "I'm living the dream!" He had time to do the things he loved and was elated at how much more time he could devote to me.

People began to ask me if he had gone back to school once he re-

> I asked him about this odd practice, and he confirmed he had put MAMS after his name. It stood for Mary Anne's Man Slave.

tired, because they noticed designation letters next to his name on his emails. I asked him about this odd practice, and he confirmed he had put *MAMS* after his name. It stood for *Mary Anne's Man Slave*. I could not stop laughing.

How could the head of our household—the strongest man I had ever met and a leader in his own right—be so devoted and eager to love and serve me? He loved me to perfection, in the way he had vowed all those many years before.

I was the one living the dream.

On November 13, 2011, that beautiful dream became a nightmare.

chapter four
A Nightmare Unfolded

P salm 23:1 begins with the words, *"Because the Lord is my Shepherd; I have everything I need."*[3]

When I awoke early on Sunday morning, November 12, 2011, I glanced over to see our granddaughter Chloe nestled asleep between the two of us. We had arranged a sleep over, which inevitably translated into a "sleep with."

I remember thinking about how much God had blessed us. We had experienced Scripture first hand. *We had everything we needed.* We had what many other couples only dreamed of—unconditional love and contentment in our marriage and our lives as a whole. We had no "wants." We were experiencing spectacular bonuses we were always thankful for. My thoughts turned to our other grandchildren and how fortunate we had been, and would be, to have the

---

3 TLB.

opportunity to repeat this scenario with all of them, over and over again.

I rallied the troops and we began our usual Sunday routine of Michael making breakfast and giving me a continual countdown of how much time was left before we had to leave for church. It was a spectacular Sunday. We proudly brought Chloe to church, and I was elated to take up a great portion of one of the back pews with two more of our grandchildren, Kale and Layla, along with my daughter, Angela, and her husband, Casey.

Michael always held me close, even in church. I generally received a couple whispered I-love-you's, a kiss on the forehead, and a couple of hand squeezes to humorously tell me I should be convicted by what the Pastor was saying.

Layla was just a baby, and there were times I thought Michael actually prayed she would become fussy so he would have the opportunity to take her to the back to rock her. His prayers were answered, and he spent most of the service that day in sheer delight, rocking her to sleep. He later told me, with very stern certainty, that no one could calm her like he could. According to him, she and he had their own special language. I seem to recall him telling me that about the other grandchildren also, but who was I to argue?

The day just kept getting better. We took Chloe home and found ourselves at Angela and Casey's for dinner. Our entire day and evening had been spent surrounded by what we valued most: our faith and our family.

Don't Come until You're Ready

That evening we chose to relax. I was so overflowing with delight from the day that I felt inspired to write. I positioned myself close to Michael so we could still have that feeling of being "together," and I wrote while he watched TV. After a couple hours of nodding and denying he was falling asleep, Michael rose and came over to hug and kiss me. I knew he was heading to bed, so I gladly began shutting everything down, but he insisted I keep writing until I was tired. He hugged and kissed me and said, "Don't come until you're ready."

That one sentence would haunt me in the months to come after that.

I never liked it when one of us went to bed without the other, so it wasn't very long before I headed down the hall to join him. I knew he wouldn't be fully asleep until I was nestled close to him, and as we cuddled I saw him smile and he did what he had done hundreds of times before. He opened my hand and ran his fingers every so softly across my palm and fingers. He had told me years before that it was his special way of telling me he was falling asleep loving me.

I closed my eyes and felt safe, loved, complete.

The Nightmare Begins

At just after 1:00 AM, I awoke startled, as if an alarm had gone off. I rolled over and noticed Michael experiencing very laboured breathing. Instinctively, I understood what was happening. I ran around to him and started screaming his name. "Michael! Michael, open your eyes! Look at me!" I could feel the panic. It was then, as I looked down at him, that I witnessed the last of his life's breath leave his body.

> I ran around to him and started screaming his name.

I screamed his name even louder. I grabbed the phone to dial 911 while I begged God for this not to be happening.

The 911 operator told me to drag him out of bed onto the floor to begin CPR. I tried, but I couldn't. His dead weight was too much for me.

I begged God even more, "please help me! I need you *now*, God!" The operator assured me they were on the way, so the only thing I could think to do was call my son-in-law Casey with my cell phone, because he was only two minutes away. Surely he had the strength.

Casey arrived before the ambulance and began CPR and mouth-to-mouth. It was at that moment that I sensed the shadow had begun moving in. It was like a crushing wave in the moments just before you realize you are going to drown. The ambulance arrived, and I will never forget how numb I felt as Casey hugged me while I prayed. I remember pacing the floors as the paramedics worked on him in our bedroom. It was as if I was trying to run ahead of what was coming, as if I could outrun the pain.

After what seemed like an eternity, I saw them bringing Michael out on a stretcher and realized they had resuscitated him. They told me to follow them to the hospital, so I sent Casey home to get Angela and call our other daughters, and I then called our closest friends. I knew they would start praying immediately and Glen would drive me to the hospital.

"I'm Taking Him Home"

The short drive seemed to take an eternity. It was comforting hearing Glen's prayers. I knew he had seen God work in mighty ways during the years he and Janette had been in ministry, and his words were strong and powerful. He was claiming a miraculous victory in this and believed it to be so.

I wanted to believe it too. However, his words began to be muffled to my hearing and the still small voice that had made itself known to me so many years before quietly engulfed me, as if to shield me from the shock as I heard God tell me: *I'm taking him home.*

Surely this couldn't be true. I must have heard God wrong. After all, Michael had died right there in our bed; if God wanted to take him home, why did He allow him to come back? Shock was beginning to take hold, and I felt more helpless than I had ever felt in my life. Surely God knew this would be a pain

I would not be able to bear. My husband, my best friend, the one single person who loved me more than life itself, was totally in God's hands now. All I could do was wait.

They began working diligently on Michael. Blood work, tests, scans. The doctor then told me Michael was unable to respond, but he was not sure if it was permanent. They told me the injury to his brain was like a bruise and they would pack him on ice to prevent it from getting worse until they could assess him further. He remained that way the following day, and I rallied every ounce of faith and trust I ever had in God and prayed the situation would change.

> I rallied every ounce of faith and trust I ever had in God and prayed the situation would change.

I knew by now people were praying. Our Elders came in to anoint him and claim a miracle, but in the back of my mind all I could hear was, *I'm taking him home, Mary Anne.*

The following day they took Michael off ice and the doctor told me that, even though he was technically breathing on his own, they would leave the breathing tubes in and bring him out of the sedation to see if he was able to respond. I prayed with all the faith I had. It was the type of praying that almost hurts because the force behind it is so intense. "Please, God, let him open his eyes and tell me he loves me one more time. Let him be okay."

> I took his face in my hands and started to break down.

When he came to and I stared into those beautiful blue eyes, I felt hopeful. His mouth was full of tubes, so I wasn't expecting him to talk, but I just wanted to see his arms move, just a signal that he could respond. I drew close to him and explained where he was and what had happened. I kissed every inch of his face. I told him I loved him more than my words could exclaim. I asked him to move his fingers, or maybe his toes, but nothing happened. I saw life in his now opened eyes, and the doctor encouraged me to talk to him and ask him questions.

I took his face in my hands and started to break down. "Look at me, Michael. I know you have seen God and He has spoken to you. Are you coming back to me?" It was then I saw tears running down his cheek and I knew the words I heard were true. God was going to take him.

I called the girls in to see him. I'm not sure why, but I wanted them to be able to see him with his eyes open. I thought somehow it would comfort them, because in my heart I knew what was ahead of us. A very short period of time afterwards, Michael began convulsing. It became so severe that they asked me to leave the room and they were forced to sedate him once again.

My heart was breaking and I could feel the shadow moving in. I was trying to stay strong for my family, but it was getting tougher by the minute.

That evening the doctor asked to speak to me privately. He ushered me to a small room where we would be alone and out of the ear shot of anyone else. We sat down facing each other, and he drew his chair in close enough to be able to take my hand. I felt the warmth of the tears that had begun descending down my cheeks. I could sense there was something more than just an update on Michael's situation. He told me it was very evident, with all he had seen of our prayers and faith, that we were believers.

For this reason he had decided to convey something he normally wouldn't.

He proceeded to say he wished he could tell me that Michael had experienced a heart attack, or stroke, or some other medical crisis that had caused this; however, that wasn't the case. As he looked into my eyes, he explained that there are times where, for no apparent reason, the signal in your brain that tells your heart to beat just shuts off. Like a light switch. As if God just decides it's time. It's called a sudden cardiac arrest. The heart just stops.

He then relayed how they would be able to keep Michael alive in hopes that there would possibly be a slight improvement, but the chances were slim, and as his wife, I was the only one who would know if that would be what Michael would want.

I couldn't control my emotions. *Oh God, please, no! Don't give me the burden of making this decision.*

I knew without a doubt what Michael would want. We had just had a conversation about it a few short weeks before this. It was as if God had prepared us. I knew what he wanted, but how could I possibly let him go?

Letting Go

The doctor could see my exhaustion and total despair. He suggested I go home and get some sleep.

Michael was sedated and nothing would happen tonight. We would talk in the morning. I was relieved at his suggestion, as I wanted our children to sleep also. They would all need their strength for what was before us.

I went home and barely had the strength to get out of my clothes. I took Michael's robe and wrapped myself in it as I laid my head on his pillow. I could smell his scent. My only comfort was that I knew he was still alive and for this night he would remain that way. I couldn't sleep, and my prayers were only for strength and comfort for my children. How would we bear this?

The following morning I felt nothing but pain in anticipation of what I would be called to do. I begged God to help me, to help me to do what was best for Michael, no matter the cost. It gave clear meaning to *Your will, not mine, Lord.*[4]

---

4 Mark 14:36.

I was relieved that it took a few hours for the doctor to reach me. When a nurse called me into a small side room and I saw the doctor with papers to sign, I felt as though my heart would stop. I asked for time to go in and speak to Michael, even though I knew he couldn't respond. I had to tell him what I was about to do; he should know. I loved and respected him too much not to.

The decision was made. He would be taken off the breathing apparatus. I signed the papers for no resuscitation. I felt as though I had signed my own death certificate, because my life would be over without him.

> I saw the doctor with papers to sign and I felt as though my heart would stop.

The doctor explained that because Michael was still capable of breathing on his own it could be an hour, a day, a week, or a month. There was no way of knowing. But I knew God would not delay this. I often think Michael's resuscitation was a gift for my children to be able to say goodbye.

I Have One Last Request

I had one request of the doctor and nurses. Once all the equipment was removed, I wanted to be able to lay in bed with Michael one last time. I wanted to feel him next to me, our hearts beating in tandem with each other. I was now living the final moments of that vow I had made nearly thirty years before—till death do us part. They were so kind and considerate. The nurses even positioned him so I would be able to drape his arms around me.

The doctor had mentioned that even though he was sedated there was a possibility he could hear us. I wanted everything he heard before he took that glorious first step into Heaven to be loving and filled with all the things he loved and cherished the most.

I told him everything I loved and admired about him. How I truly felt he was the greatest husband and father that ever lived. How I had learned so much of what a godly man was by watching how he lived his life and treated me. I mentioned that God must have felt he was extremely special to actually fulfill his wish for the exact way he wanted to "relocate" from earth to Heaven—in his sleep, effortlessly.

I sang him some songs, kissed his lips, touched his face, and actually fell asleep next to him. When I awoke I knew it was time for our children and our grandson Mackenzie to come in and say their goodbyes.

Hours later, in the wee hours of the morning, I gathered with my family and Glen and Janette as we sang Michael's favourite hymns and told him how much we loved him.

At 4:20 AM on November 17, God took Michael's hand and welcomed him home.

chapter five

The Valley of the Shadow

I left the hospital that morning somewhat in shock and disbelief. I had heard what God told me, but somewhere deep within my breaking heart I had hoped He would change his mind.

I'm not totally certain I can clearly explain what I was feeling, but it was as if the internal clock of my life had frozen. There were no more minutes, no more moments in time—only stillness held tight by a concrete vice of pain and despair.

It was then I first recognized it. The shadow was very real. It was much like the looming, creeping darkness that fills the sky and our surroundings the moments before a terrifying thunder and lightning storm. I stood before the window of my life and watched as the spectre filled every encompassing space with an ambiguous reality of what was now before me.

I had now stepped into *The Valley of the Shadow of Death*, and I had no strength to climb out of it.

Other people I had loved dearly in my life had died. My parents, some friends, colleagues, but nothing even remotely compared to this.

In Mark 10:7–8 Scripture tells us, *"For this reason a man will leave his father and mother ... and the two will become one flesh."*[5] I felt as though I, too, had died. We were one and we had been torn apart. Nothing looked or felt the same.

Comprehension of the term "shadow of death" became clear. There was now a dark-ness separating me from everything and everyone around me, even though I was still able to see through it. I could hear people's voices, feel their touch, but this new barrier held me captive to the feelings and devastation that was mine and mine alone. I was numb.

> I had now stepped into The Valley of the Shadow of Death, and I had no strength to climb out of it.

A Few Short Weeks Before

I found my mind wandering back to just a few short weeks before, when Michael and I were on vacation in Napa and we found ourselves entrenched in a long conversation about what would happen if one of us died. It was one of those occasions when I knew the details of what was being said were extremely important. Little did I know at that time just how important. We discussed our lives together, our children, our faith, and most importantly, Michael went into great explanation of every last detail of what he wanted at his funeral. I am eternally thankful for that time. It saved me from the stress of having to think even once about any of the arrangements.

The funeral was held over for nine days so that all his wishes would be fulfilled exactly as he desired, even to the point of being held on a Saturday because he didn't want anyone to have to take time off work if they chose to attend. Michael was always considerate, even to the end.

I realize now just how much shock I was in, as there are things I simply don't remember about the wake at the funeral home or his funeral. I remember the lines of friends, family, and colleagues.

Even some of the students he had impacted during his work with the VIP program in the schools came because they wanted me to know that he had been instrumental in changing and impacting their lives in some way.

The day of the funeral, I sat silently in the car with my grandson Mackenzie while being driven by one of Michael's fellow officers and friend into the parking lot at Mapleview Community Church, "our church." It was surreal. How could this be happening? Just two weeks prior, I sat with Michael in the doctor's office and heard the doctor jokingly proclaim, "I don't think I will ever need to see you again; you're one of the healthiest people I know."

I glanced up and saw the Police Honour Guard, and reality hit hard. They were there to escort and salute his casket, and that was a confirmation that Michael was inside.

I was somewhat shocked but not surprised at the hundreds of people who were there. I couldn't help but think how pleased he would have been to see them all.

Hearing (the Voice) Again

I had asked to spend just a few moments alone with Michael before the funeral started. I stared at the Canadian flag draped over his coffin and wondered what would become of me and my family now. My life with Michael was everything I had ever wanted or needed. I looked up to Heaven and begged God to put his arms around me. I can honestly say I never doubted God's reasons for taking Michael at that time; however, I was totally void of any confidence that I would survive, let alone come through this.

> I was totally void of any confidence that I would survive, let alone come through this.

I gently ran my fingers across the casket, and in that moment I recognized the feeling of God's arms cradling me. In that stark silence I heard that still small voice that had led me so many other times. *Mary Anne, hold tight to me, because deep, deep, down in that pain a plan will grow and you will understand.* God was not telling me this was what He planned for me, but He was assuring me He would take me into the next phase of my life.

It was a beautiful, moving funeral. Our children spoke with the highest level of love and respect about their father, and I was able to draw enough strength to say my final public goodbye. I ended it exactly the way we had always said goodbye. "See you later, Darling… 1… 2… 3." We even took the opportunity to sing a resounding rendition of Michael's favourite song, "Sweet Caroline." It wasn't until I heard the voices of everyone singing Michael's favourite hymn, "How Great Thou Art," that I knew I would cling to exactly that.

Then sings my soul, my Saviour God to thee, how great thou art, how great thou art. It would only be in the strength of God's greatness that I would survive.

I left the church that day feeling exhausted and more alone than I had ever been.

chapter six

The Forsaken Zone

Nothing could have prepared me for what was awaiting me. After all, everyone knew who I was—a great wife, mother, grandmother, and a professional woman who could run for hours on what appeared to be an endless supply of energy. My faith in God was limitless. I felt His presence daily in every circumstance and situation I faced. I even experienced moments of laughing with Him as I imagined what He might be thinking while I prayed He would help me parallel park. I loved and cared for my family and my grandchildren, and I was at the top of my game professionally. But that was gone! It had been replaced with a grief so deep I could barely function.

Going Through the Motions

My days were now spent going through the motions. I would spend time with my children and grandchildren, do my work, and go to church. But deep down, I had one goal, and one goal only. I would crawl into bed at night, curl up in a ball, and beg God to take me also. Michael's words haunted me daily: *Come when you're ready*. I'm ready *now*!

I was not only grieving Michael's loss, I was also so very weary. It was the first time in my life I had no strength to comfort my children. They were going through horrific pain themselves. They had lost their father, and for all appearances, they were close to losing their mother also.

I was angry with myself. I had suffered some very painful life-altering events in my time, but I always rose above, always had the stamina and faith to come through. This was different. I had lost all confidence in myself. The shadow of death had begun to morph into a darkness so intense in its fervor

> Michael's words haunted me daily: Come when you're ready. I'm ready now!

that I couldn't fight it off. And just as a thorny vine can wind its way around a beautiful plant to the point you can no longer see it, in my mind it grew so strong and thick that I could see nothing good around me. Grief was my new constant companion, my captor, and it held the upper hand.

People tried to comfort me in the best way they knew how. I knew they loved Michael and me dearly, and watching my pain through their helplessness was difficult for them. Unfortunately, as a society we are never really given guidance or instruction on handling the loss of someone or how to comfort those who have.

This is especially true in the church. It is as if there is an unwritten understanding that, because we are firm believers, somehow that will be enough to carry us through. In theory that is true; however, in the midst of loss, it is severely flawed thinking. Perhaps that is why God's Word commands us to be involved "practically" in the lives of widows and orphans.

James 1:27: *Religion that God our Father accepts as pure and faultless is this: to look after orphans and widows in their distress…*[6]

A Pile of Walking Pain

Please, don't misunderstand me. I am a strong believer who has been on the receiving end of the power of God's Word. But I have to be totally honest here—at this place and time in my life it became neither soothing nor comforting.

Every person's handling of grief and loss is different, as is what comforts them, so I can only speak for myself. When someone wanted to throw a good Christian cliché or the "perfect" Scripture my way, I felt as though I wanted to physically harm them. You know, the come-close-so-I-can-punch-you type of harm them. I am generally a very loving and kind person; however, I had become a barely functioning pile of walking pain looking for relief. It was an unusual place. I still trusted and believed in God, but I felt as though I had somehow let go of His hand and couldn't find Him to grasp it again.

Words did not comfort me.

I *did not* want to hear… *I can do all things through Christ who strengthens me.*[7]

---

7 Philippians 4:13 NKJV.

Really? Do you have any idea what I have been through in my life? I have no strength left! I know He's there—I don't doubt that—but I can't feel Him through this debilitating agony.

I *did not* want to hear... *In all things God works for the good of those who love him, who have been called according to his purpose.*[8]

Well, I had lost my husband, my best friend, my lover, my safety and security, my confidant, the spiritual leader in my household, father to my children, Papa to my grandchildren, the person who loved me unconditionally as no other person had, who made me laugh, dried my tears, encouraged me, my limitless cheerleader, my defender, the ever constant light and laughter in my life. How would this work together for my good ... hmmmm?

> I did not want God as my husband—I wanted my husband!

I *did not* want to hear... *God is a husband to the widow.*

---

8 Romans 8:28 NIV.

This would bring me to tears probably faster than anything else. When I would crawl into bed at night and sob until I nearly vomited, I did not want God as my husband—I wanted my husband!

I *wanted* to hear… *I don't know what to say, so I just want to say I Love You!*

Because I needed love.

I *wanted* to hear… *Please let me hold you and comfort you because I think this is unbearable.*

Because it was unbearable.

I *wanted* to hear… *I am praying that somehow you feel God's comfort while you're in the midst of this.*

Because more than anything else, God would be what would ultimately bring me through.

Attending church was becoming more and more difficult. Michael and I had been involved at Mapleview for nearly thirteen years by this time. We had served there in several capacities on our own, and certainly, as a couple. Michael was part of the Elders board and I had been part of ministry and support on several fronts. The people there were more like family than friends, and God was ever-present each time we were there.

Until now.

I had somehow lost Him. It was as though I couldn't remember how to get to where He was.

I Tried Desperately to Feel God

I'll never forget the Sunday I totally broke. I sat in my car in the church parking lot and thought of all the times Michael and I had walked in there, hand in hand. I was nearly frozen. How could I walk in there without him again? So much time had gone by, yet it seemed as though it was yesterday. I felt I no longer belonged—not on my own, at least. Part of me was missing, and that part rendered me no longer useful in this environment.

I knew realistically this wasn't true, but a grief-stricken mind can take you to places that appear very real. I walked into strange and *un*familiar familiarity. Again I went through the motions, but holding my tears back was more difficult than usual. I tried desperately to feel God during worship, but my heart was empty. I barely heard a word of the message and sensed a feeling of utter isolation and loss.

After my pastor finished his message and dismissed us, people began to get up and chat. I couldn't move. I felt a separation from God I had never experienced before. It was as if my grief had swallowed me whole.

> I felt a separation from God I had never experienced before. It was as if my grief had swallowed me whole.

Glen came up behind me and put his hand on my shoulder, and I broke completely. He wasn't expecting that response at all. As he came around to sit beside me, I could sense his concern. What was wrong?

I could barely speak. I looked up through the sobbing that ensued and spoke what my heart was feeling. "God has forsaken me!" He did the only thing he could: he prayed.

My heart was completely broken and my soul felt empty.

chapter seven

Familiar Words

As I drove home from church that day, I tried to reason with myself. I had been involved in grief counselling and was painfully aware that this road was not going to be easy, nor would it be over quickly. I knew there were several stages to go through, and no matter how much I wanted to rush them, there would be no way to control it. I remember the day my counsellor told me it could take as long as five years to feel as though I felt some sense of joy in living again. I thought to myself, "It won't take that long— I will never survive it."

I walked into my home feeling fiercely numb. I began walking through each room, methodically, as if searching for a clue for what my next step should be. Everything reminded me of a life I no longer had.

I felt as though I was living Psalm 22:14–15.

I am poured out like water,
and all my bones are out of joint.
My heart has turned to wax;
it has melted within me.
My mouth is dried up like a potsherd,
and my tongue sticks to the roof of my mouth;
you lay me in the dust of death.[9]

Back Where the Nightmare Began

I entered our bedroom and slowly walked in. This was the place my nightmare began that fateful night. I could feel my heart beating as though my chest would burst, and I fell to my knees, sobbing uncontrollably. It wasn't long before I found myself on the floor, curled up in a ball. I cried out to God. "Why have you forsaken me? ... I need you!"

It was then my own words surrounded my heart. It was as if my weakness was the open door to God's presence. Those were familiar words I had heard before.

---

9 NIV.

Matthew 27:46: *And about the ninth hour
Jesus cried out with a loud voice, saying,
"Eli, Eli, lama sabachthani?" that is, "My
God, My God, why have you forsaken me?*[10]

My God Moment

I sat on the floor and dried my tears. My heart was
waiting in anticipation, like a child that had fallen
and was hurt seeing their parent running toward
them to bring comfort.

Please let me assure you that I am in no way com-
paring my level of pain to what Christ went through
on the cross, but what it brought to my mind was the
fact that He bore a weight so heavy and wracked with
pain that He felt separated from everything that He
knew as the limitless love and magnificent greatness
that was God. Yet, three days later He was the man-
ifestation of the greatest love and victory the world
had ever known or seen.

God had not forsaken me—He hadn't even let go
of my hand! He was carrying me as I lay in His arms
in a state of spiritual unconsciousness brought about

---

10 NKJV.

> God had not forsaken me—He hadn't even let go of my hand!

by my loss. I was still afraid. I was still unsure of how I would survive this, but I was not alone.

I didn't realize this was to be my first step out from under the shadow of death and toward the safety of His guidance. There were no fireworks, no special messages or signs, but what I felt was the familiar feeling of God's presence—not just head knowledge but heart knowledge.

I had to reach outside the shadow, outside the pain, and draw nourishment from the place my trust in God lived. The survivor I had always been was crawling through a desert on her hands and knees, thirsty and weak. My only source of strength would be to drink from the well of the living waters only God could give me. I was starving for Him.

I thought of parts of Psalm 63:

O God, you are my God,
and I long for you.
My whole being desires you;
like a dry, worn-out, and waterless land,

my soul is thirsty for you.
Let me see you in the sanctuary;
let me see how mighty and glorious you are.
Your constant love is better than life itself,
and so I will praise you.
I will give you thanks as long as I live;
I will raise my hands to you in prayer.
My soul will feast and be satisfied,
and I will sing glad songs of praise to you.
As I lie in bed, I remember you;
all night long I think of you,
because you have always been my help.
In the shadow of your wings I sing for joy.
I cling to you,
and your hand keeps me safe. [11]

In Genesis 16:13 when Hagar was suffering in the desert, she refers to Him as "The God who sees me."[12] I knew He saw me also. He always had. When I longed for my mother to love me, God loved me. When I was terrified at the hands of my grandfather, He calmed me. When I was betrayed as a young wife

---

11 Psalm 63:1–8 GNT.

12 NLT.

and mother, He comforted me. Why would He not be with me now?

I Felt the Need to Repent

When I climbed under the covers that night, instead of crying myself to sleep, I was longing for the familiarity of peace. I quieted my mind and rested. I let my thoughts drift to the times I had physically felt God. I wouldn't allow even the slightest diversion from it. I confessed my innermost thoughts. Good and bad. Although I knew He understood what I had gone through emotionally, I felt the

> That night, instead of crying myself to sleep, I was longing for the familiarity of peace.

need to repent. Were there times I had been unreasonable? I had asked to die; was that unforgivable? I knew it wasn't, but I wanted Him to know I was disappointed in myself. I was not only missing Michael—I was missing God terribly also.

I felt a sense of release. But more importantly, I felt the Holy Spirit draw near. I knew I was His child and He cradled me. I didn't want it to end. I fell into the deepest sleep I had experienced in months.

I wish I could tell you I awoke the next morning a totally emotionally healed person. But I wasn't. I still had to go through grief and I was feeling so very confused. I was constantly asking God questions, but the difference was I knew and felt He was guiding me along step by step.

The questions that haunted me continually were *Who are you now? Where do you belong? What do you do from here forward?*

I wanted the old me back, but that wasn't possible. The old me had been part of a couple my entire adult life. There wasn't a single interaction in my life that hadn't changed as a result of this. Even my focus with God had changed. There was a piece missing, and not only could I not find it, I didn't know where to begin to look.

A few weeks later, Mapleview was hosting our District Pastors Conference and Pastors Tommy and Matthew Barnett were coming in from the US to be the leaders and teachers. The word went out for volunteers to help facilitate, and I thought perhaps this would be a fresh distraction for me. Who wouldn't want to hear about their ministry and the Dream Centre?

A God-Ordained Moment

I was assigned to help at the book table (go figure), which pleased me to no end, because it put me right into the middle of the conference at all times. I was running into people I hadn't seen in years, and it wasn't long before I understood this was a God-ordained appointment. I hadn't written a word since Michael died, but being at the table, browsing through the books, began to bring back a familiar feeling of creativity. It was exciting and moving to hear all that these pastors were doing for the homeless and disenfranchised in Los Angeles, and there was hope in their words.

On the final day of the conference, both Tommy and Matthew announced they would be praying for needs, clarity of purpose, and ministry for those attending who wanted it. "This couldn't be better timing," I thought. Surely this was why I had come there. After all, who needed it more than I did?

The room was crowded. However, I was positioned perfectly to be close to the front of the line.

I quickly moved around the table, but as I was meandering through the group of pastors, all of a sudden I felt a hesitation. I wasn't hesitating because I was afraid or because I couldn't make my way to the front; I stopped because I felt it coming … first the feeling of being engulfed and set apart … and then I heard it, once again—that still small voice.

Don't go up, Mary Anne, you don't need it.

> It's you and Me.
> That's all you need—
> you and Me.

"*What?* I know You're God and all, but let's look at this. If anyone needs these prayers, it's me. I am definitely in need, I have no clarity of purpose, and what would my ministry be going forward?" I felt as though I was the only person in the room when I heard Him next.

It's you and Me. That's all you need—you and Me.

I was delighted, as always, to hear from God (it's like a hug to my spirit), but I was even more confused. "You and Me, Lord? That sounds like the beginnings of a plan, but I am nowhere near understanding who *me* is anymore."

I knew who God was, but it was as if I was sensing Him peripherally. But on the other hand, something was changing in me. I wanted to go to Him—not in death as I had previously been asking—but in life.

Hang On to Your Hat!

That night I calmly talked to God. I couldn't help but feel it was more like a follow-up meeting. I needed to express how I was feeling, and I was certain He was going to be okay with that. After all, He was the one who had started it.

"You and Me? If all I will need is my faith in You for the next step, then please show me where You are, exactly where You are. And for goodness sake, show me who I am."

Knowing what I do now, I can picture God smiling and whispering, *Hang on to your hat, Mary Anne. Are you ever going to be surprised!*

chapter eight

Words that Speak

One of the characteristics of God I love the most is His eagerness to meet us where we are at and in exactly the way we will feel and understand Him the most intensely. I have seen the look of questioning on people's faces when I have relayed a story of where or how I have heard from God, and some have commented that they would never look for Him in those places or in those ways. Of course they wouldn't—they're not me and God knows that. If you're serious, He'll be in your seriousness; if you're reserved, He'll be directly in the centre of your holding back and restraint.

Hugging Fifty-Two Strangers

He understands I am very relational and sensory. I feel very deeply, especially for someone in distress, sadness, or need. Connecting with people for the sole purpose of making them feel valued is one of

> One of the character-istics of God I love the most is His eagerness to meet us where we are at and in exactly the way we will feel and understand Him the most intensely.

my greatest pleasures in life. In fact, I challenge myself to hug fifty-two strangers a year (one each week) to that end.

My creative and visual nature makes me prone to seeing great meaning and interpretation in animate and inanimate objects, places, and situations. Gazing at a building or a painting for an hour will evoke an enormous variety of thoughts, even revelations, and a journey through the full spectrum of emotions.

It was no surprise to me that God knew exactly the way the message needed to be delivered and what I needed to hear and see at this crossroads in my life.

In 2010, through the magical world of Facebook I became part of some of the groups from the neighbourhood in which I had grown up and gone to school in Southwest Detroit. I already had connections and sustained friendships with some of my childhood friends, but this really broadened the re-kindling of friendships with people I hadn't seen for more than four decades.

Back to My Roots

I can't say exactly when, but sometime in 2014, I began seeing posts about St. Vincent (my high school) having an all years reunion. Up until then, since Michael's death I had only crossed into the Detroit area on my way to Frankenmuth to meet up for a girl's weekend with two of my most cherished childhood friends, Val and Norbel. Even that was difficult, but being with them was easy. I could break down whenever I needed to, and the love we had felt for each other since childhood was overflowing and unconditional even now.

But my high school reunion? That would be a whole different story.

Friends began to inquire as to whether I would be going. My heart was longing to see everyone, but I was fearful on several levels. It wasn't the usual high school reunion jitters about getting older or not recognizing people—it was other things.

First of all, with the exception of being at a couple of weddings with my children, this would be the first time I would be attending a social function alone, without Michael, as a single woman. This was very foreign territory for me. I knew it would happen sooner or later, but four-and-a-half hours away from home, on my own, was not exactly how I pictured that first time to be.

Venturing Out

Second was the fact that the only thing worse than my parallel parking is my sense of direction, and to go would mean driving around Detroit by myself. Now, I know I have travelled extensively across Canada and the US due to work for a number of years, but I was always in familiar territory or had a driver to take me where I needed to go and back again. This, however, would be *Detroit*, and this, would be *alone*!

And then a more prevalent fear set in. What if someone asked me about Michael and I broke down, right there in front of everyone? Would they think I was weak? Would they understand? Would they back away? Could I really take that chance?

I prayed for courage (and that the Google Maps App would not fail me) and made a commitment to attend.

The drive there was filled with reminiscent Motown music and thoughts of all that had transpired in my life since high school. I cried a good portion of the way, I think mostly as a release of all the mixed emotions I was feeling. As I waited in my car to clear US Customs at the Ambassador Bridge, I felt a warm sense of familiarity as I looked to the right and saw the abandoned Metro Detroit Train Depot.

"What a magnificent old girl she is," I thought. Certainly one of my most favourite buildings in all of Detroit.

I couldn't help but think that the building that was once my high school still stood kitty corner from her on 14th Street. The small three-story building at 2020 14th Street housed the events and times of the people that I had driven so far now to see. I began sensing that coming here was the right decision.

Once I checked into my hotel, my cell phone began ringing, and for the next twenty-four hours I was able to do some catching up with people before the actual reunion, which helped relax me before going.

The first few moments inside the hall where the reunion was held brought back some feelings I hadn't expected or was totally prepared for. In my book *Before I Knew You Loved Me,* I penned these words about being a total stranger integrated into my high school.

Although I was spending time in a depressed area of Detroit, I somehow felt as though I really belonged there. My new friends understood alcoholism, drug addiction, violence, and how dreams were vulnerable to being squashed by outside circumstances. They were like me: victims of prejudices and deep dark secrets.[13]

Of course they would understand. Nothing had changed.

The Uniting Force

As I perused the room, I remembered the uniting force that had been forged between us many years before. As I felt the first touch, the first hug, the first gentle kiss to my cheek in the initial moments of greeting everyone, I was engulfed by the feeling that even

> I somehow felt as though I really belonged there. My new friends understood

13 Mary Anne Moran, *Before I Knew You Loved Me* (Word Alive Press, 2008), p. 27.

> You can't explain our friendship. It just was, and still is, entrenched in who we are.

though our smiles had aged, our love hadn't. I have often told people you can't explain Detroit—you just *are* Detroit. In much the same way, you can't explain our friendship. It just was, and still is, entrenched in who we *are*. I had nothing to fear. I was home.

The evening was a raving success. I had opportunity to see my best friend, Shirley, sporting our cheerleading sweater, and all the pictures from the past were endearing. There were friends there whose impact is felt on my life even still today, along with previous boyfriends, memories of my first kiss, broken hearts, and a million laughs over high school shenanigans. I felt relaxed for the first time in a very long time. Little did I know, God had just pulled back the first layer that would expose the true meaning of why I was there.

I have a friend named Josie who is an event organizer extraordinaire. There is nothing she loves more than friends coming together to visit and support each other. (In fact, she gathered those of us who started grade 9 together in 1969 to celebrate our sixtieth birthdays this past summer.) It wasn't a surprise that Josie felt the reunion evening just wasn't enough and that we should gather for a "goodbye for now" lunch at a restaurant before some of us started our long drives home. Although I wanted to go, I hesitated. It was Sunday and I had a five-hour drive home. However, I couldn't shake the feeling that I should be there.

An Emotional Vacation

As I drove to the lunch, I began dreading going home. It was as if I had been on an emotional vacation.

I would be going back to all the reminders of the uncertainty of my life and who I was—or more so, who I no longer was. My motivating factor to return was, of course, my children and grandchildren, but I feared my grief was becoming burdensome to them also.

I tried to give myself a pep talk, which turned into a personal scolding. I looked at my eyes in the rear-view mirror and said, "Mary Anne, you are an adult, a professional. You made it here this weekend and look how great it turned out. Take a step

> I tried to give myself a pep talk, which turned into a personal scolding.

forward, show God you are ready." But I wasn't ready. That big question still loomed out there. Who am I, and what's the plan?

This wasn't just any lunch; God had arranged every moment for the exact desired effect and outcome. Friends were there who had been unable to be at the reunion. If I had not gone I wouldn't have seen them. I sat close to Maria, whose words of encouragement about God's grace filled my heart. To this day God uses her to minister to me. The only seat empty for me to take was next to Tom Valdez. We had already had a wonderful conversation at the reunion about his beautiful wife, his sons, and where life had taken him since high school. He was very kind in the way he asked me about my life, and in particular, about Michael. I felt comfortable talking about it and was surprised I hadn't shed a tear.

We took the last of our group pictures and began to get up to say goodbye. That was when Tom reached over, looked directly and intently into my eyes, and took my hand. It was very much reminiscent of many years ago, after I had moved away, when I would visit my parents and at the moments just previous to leaving my father would take my hand in a last attempt to convey a deep and meaningful message before I left for home. Tom smiled and said, "Mary Anne, I want you to know how very happy we all are that *you* came."

At that moment, I felt as though time had stopped. That short endearing declaration opened my mind— and more importantly, my heart—wide open. God had spoken directly to me through him. This was the reason I had come!

When Tom said "*You*," God rolled back the shadow and said, *Now it is time to remember … remember the you that was, and still is, mine.* I could feel a sense much like warm, refreshing water rinsing off an enormous burden of pain.

We said our goodbyes, made promises to see each other soon, and headed to the parking lot.

The Unfolding Plan

As I sat in my car, I could feel the floodgate of tears open wide. These were not the same tears I had shed for grief—these were tears of thankfulness. I was remembering the *you* that was *me*.

The *you* that was *me* before my grief and loss... God had a plan.

The *you* that was *me* before I was a wife...God had a plan.

The *you* that was *me* before I was a mother... God had a plan.

The *you* that was *me* before I suffered pain and trauma as a child...God had a plan.

The *you* that was *me* before I survived my mother's difficult pregnancy and my subsequent premature birth as a baby they had warned her not to have... God had a plan.

I couldn't help but think of Psalm 139:13–14.

For you formed my inward parts; you wove me in my mother's womb. I will give thanks to you, for I am fearfully and wonderfully made.[14]

I turned my car on, and as always, reached for the radio. Unbeknownst to me, it was tuned in to a Christian radio station, and I listened to a song I hadn't previously heard–"The Great Unfolding" by

---

14 ESV.

Steven Curtis Chapman. It was a love song from God to me, with a message of precise direction.

> *"If we just keep on believing… the story is so far from over"*[15]

While I sat there, gripping my steering wheel and drinking in every word, God graciously put His arms around me and said, *I don't want you to merely survive, Mary Anne, I want you to thrive!* Just like the words of the song said, God knew this was not how I thought my life would be; and yet, He also knew there was a plan from the start and that His promises to me were true.

I remembered God's address and I was headed straight for His house.

I dried my tears, put my car in drive, and knew exactly where I needed to go. I remembered God's address and I was headed straight for His house.

---

15 Steven Curtis Chapman, "Glorious Unfolding" © 2013 One Blue Petal Music / Primary Wave Brian (BMI) All rights admin. by Wixen Music.

God's house.

7060 McGraw

Pulling up in front of 7060 McGraw, I half expected the front doors to burst open and see God running to welcome me. I got out of my car and headed to the front doors of St. Andrews Church. I had so hoped to be able to stand inside, but the doors were locked. I walked around the perimeter, peeking and peering into every window possible before sitting down outside to reflect. I knew I was smiling.

When I was very young I was told this was God's house, and I took that literally. When we would have the occasion to attend another church for weddings, funerals, etc., the environment and service were familiar; however, I believed I knew where God actually lived, so I thought the other places must be where He vacations.

I needed to be there, because this was the very first place I had ever heard Him. My thoughts drifted back to that little girl praying for a miracle and hearing God say, *You already have the miracle, Mary Anne. The miracle is that you belong to me.* I hadn't understood those words then, but I certainly did now. I did "belong" to Him, not as a possession to be used at whim but in the sense that I was a part of all that He was. He was as intricately woven into my life as I was into His. Standing there gave me the assurance that He had been with me every step of the way, even when my pain was so intense that I couldn't remember His address.

I didn't want to leave, but I knew I would be back. I felt like Joshua getting ready to invade Canaan, when God spoke and said, *I will always be with you, I will never abandon you. Be determined and confident.*[16]

Saying Goodbye to My Past

On my way home, I decided to make some stops in Windsor. Sort of a goodbye to some of my past. I stopped in front of the house where my grandfather had succeeded in halting any semblance of me experiencing a normal childhood, where he had hurt me and scarred me for life. I felt unusually calm, as the same sensation of warmth covered me, and I knew even this would not thwart my future.

Next, I stopped in front of the house in which I lived when I was first married, and I remembered how my dreams of all that life would be were wiped out by my first husband and his mistress. Again, the warmth surrounded me and I said goodbye.

Next stop was the last home I had ever visited my mother in. I wished we could have been so much more to each other but remembered how faithful God had been in healing our relationship. I said goodbye.

---

16 Joshua 1:5b–6a GNT.

Driving home, I was exhausted from emotion but was feeling something I thought I had lost—hope. I knew I would still be struggling with grief and loss, but at least now I felt there was something waiting for me. There was a purpose and a plan. I sensed I would return soon, as God had much more to show me.

And He did...

chapter nine

Up, Down, and All Around

I arrived home after that fateful weekend with a renewed purpose in life. God hadn't revealed what that would be, but I was confident He would continue to hold my hand along the way. I still suffered from sustained times of loneliness and loss, but I understood this was a very natural process to go through. There were times I wondered if the people around me would consider either shooting me or having me committed, as I was being ruled by my emotions and they were up and down and all around every corner available. But I was literally "finding" myself, and that wasn't easy.

I decided to take some of the pressure off, and since I knew God was wide open to speaking to me, I began to ask questions and journal His answers. I was also very aware that the bigger the plan God has for your life, the more opposition you will get from the opposing forces of the enemy. I had to keep myself afloat in the midst of that opposition.

Reinventing Myself

Many of you reading this have been through tremendous loss or pain yourselves, and the natural reaction is to want relief from that pain as quickly and painlessly as possible. I understand this, for I also longed for it, but what I have found to be true is that great intention and drive of purpose are actually forged and born through the loss. I wanted to feel "normal" but realized, just as it says in Song of Solomon, *"I slept, but my heart was awake."*[17] Through this journey, my mind was in a sleep-like state, overcome with exhaustion, but my heart was awake as it had always been, broken but waiting to be healed.

Albert Camus wrote, "In the depth of winter, I finally learned that within me there lay an invincible summer."

I let the reigns of grief go so it would run ahead of me so far into the distance that I would not see it. I would live knowing there would never be a day it would not somehow remain intertwined in my life, but now a new and different force began to

---

17 Song of Solomon 5:2 NLT.

pull me. And as Albert Camus wrote, *"In the depth of winter, I finally learned that within me there lay an invincible summer."*[18]

It didn't take me long to realize that, even though I had managed companies, lectured extensively on nutrition and nutritional products, and served in leadership, I had no idea how to re-invent myself in my new life circumstances. So I decided to tackle it much the same way I would dive into a new business venture.

I first looked back at what had transpired since Michael had relocated to Heaven. I had made what I considered some mistakes, led primarily by pain, and had to forgive myself. I also had to let go of hurtful feelings concerning the people I thought had let me down during that time. I knew there were things I had expected that they were just unable to give, and I was confident that those who acted in an unfeeling or insensitive manner would someday understand what they could have done differently.

I also realized that previously when I thought about what made up Mary Anne Moran as a person,

---

18 Albert Camus in *Lyrical and Critical Essays*, Vintage Books Edition, Ed. Philip Thoday and Trans. Ellen Conroy Kennedy (New York: Albert A. Knopf, 1970), p. 169.

those qualities usually revolved around what I was as a wife and mother. I had been in that role so long that I had forgotten what actually makes up the total composition of who I am.

I thought perhaps I would join all the pieces of this puzzle and be able to visualize the big picture of where I was heading. The unexpected part was the realization of what I had forgotten along the way.

The Importance of Counselling

At this time I would like to stress the importance of receiving counselling when you have experienced loss of any type, but especially when that loss is through death. I know God is our comfort and guide, but He has given people professional gifts for a purpose. Personally, I don't believe it is in our physical or spiritual nature to be able to cope with grief. After all, we were never meant to. As far as I know, when God created Adam and Eve there was never meant to be death, so in my humble opinion I don't think our minds were ever given a coping mechanism for this. Perhaps that is why there is so much reference in Scripture to God "bringing us through." We can't handle it on our own.

I was fortunate enough to have been connected with a grief counsellor who has turned out to be a very dear and loving friend. Faye asked me all the tough questions. She asked not only about my feelings of grief but also about circumstances and thought patterns I had developed over a lifetime. Partially through her, God was pulling the pieces of my re-invention together. I just hadn't realized it.

I was sure God was chuckling as I began to journal specifics about myself in hopes of gaining a greater sense of who I actually was outside the wife and mother role. I would write things down and then tell Him, as if He didn't already know.

Of course, I started with what I felt were my hindrances to progression. I realized I was a bit (well, actually, a lot) of a control person—hence, my continued frustration in not being further along with my grief process—and I had a tendency to stuff my feelings. This is not a good combo. Then there is the fact that behind these smiling Irish eyes is a mostly dormant temper that, much like a volcano, erupts at the worst possible times when put under tremendous pressure. Fortunately, the occasions of this happening are few and far between.

Learning to Trust People All Over Again

I was also finding it difficult to trust people. I hadn't needed to trust anyone except Michael. I could bring any situation or problem to him, and because of his love for me I knew he had my best interest at heart. He wasn't like the other people I had loved, who had hurt me or let me down. I decided, for now, I would put my trust in God and He would have to guide and teach me.

One of the unusual side effects of my grief was my loss of confidence. God had to remind me of my greatest gifts and talents. He also had to remind me that this would be a process, and He frequently did this right in His old neighbourhood.

God Lives in Detroit

I found myself longing to go to Detroit more and more ... and who wouldn't? I laughed there, I was loved tremendously there, and I was fed more delicious food there than one person could possibly consume. But more than this, I looked forward to hearing from God. I realize I had a wonderful relationship with Him daily, but this had become our "special" place, much like a particular favourite meeting spot where you and your closest friend can talk with reck-

> I was loved tremendously there, and I was fed more delicious food there than one person could possibly consume.

less abandon about the deepest issues of life or simply enjoy each other's company without interruption.

As mentioned previously, God knows exactly how to meet me with messages formed in the perfection of a place, object, or event. Detroit provided every visual I needed. I had discovered with each visit that I would eventually find myself standing directly at a location awaiting words from Him that both inspired and healed me.

The first time this happened, I stood admiringly in front of the old Metro Detroit Train Depot.[19] This is one of my most treasured buildings in all of Detroit. At first, I reflected on how magnificent she was in her day. As I looked at the splendor and monumental beauty of her architecture, I could imagine

---

19 "Michigan Central Station" is the official name of this building, while "Metro Detroit Train Depot" is the locally used moniker.

the hustle and bustle of passengers, and the business that transpired within her walls. She had been hostess to presidents, celebrities, and some very notable and famous Americans.

I then grew somewhat sad as I looked at what she was now—abandoned; areas crumbling from wear, abandonment, and neglect; graffiti and barbed wire encompassing her exterior.

Michigan Central Station

"Look Deeper"

It was then I could hear God tell me, *Look deeper …
you haven't seen it yet.* As I gazed closely, I saw that
even though she was not operating in her initial capac-
ity she still remained strong. Even the graffiti could
not cover the beauty and intricacy of her Beaux-Arts
classical architecture, both inside and out.

Was that true of myself also? Although I felt
abandoned and crumbling, the beauty in my soul
still remained. It maintained its strength. That was
evident in what others saw in me.

My eyes turned to the barbed wire and I no longer thought of it as a sign of defeat but rather as res-
cuing arms that were keeping her safe until she was
once again at a place of being restored. This is what
God had done for me. He was protecting me when I
lacked the strength or resources to protect myself.

I spoke to God and thanked Him for this beautiful visual but asked what this had to do with me
moving forward. He said, *You still haven't seen it.* I
perused the exterior more closely. Then I looked up
and noticed the reconstruction work being done to
her. There were new windows being put in! Someone
had realized she still had worth and had taken the

first steps to "bring her back." Because of what she had been through, it would have to be done bit by bit, in a manner she could tolerate. She would never be the same, but she had the potential

> Someone had realized she still had worth and had taken the first steps to "bring her back."

to be whatever someone believed she could be, magnificent once again.

This was precisely what God was executing within me, in stages I could tolerate. He was bringing His plan for my fulfilling my life into place, one step at a time.

My Street Resembled a War Zone

Many months later, a good friend took me to the street where I grew up. Originally this was for curiosity purposes only. My street resembled a war zone. We saw crumbled, dilapidated houses, but all signs of most of the old thriving businesses were gone. Some of the shells of the businesses and some signage remained, but they were devoid of any life within their walls.

Only the shells of businesses remained.

I decided to get out and stroll up the street. I was running scenarios in my mind of times spent playing with friends or walking to school, our corner bakery, Tarnow Park, or of course, my favourite, Karas's candy store. I wished it was all still there. I longed to hear my friends, smell familiar smells, and simply gaze upon people's lives as I had known them. I looked at the details of each house carefully as I passed and realized I had begun to sense God's presence. When I arrived at the corner, I turned to look back. It was then I comprehended that, even though some of the houses were gone, all the trees were still there. It was because they had rooted so deeply that not even the events of evil, despair, and destruction had taken them down.

Tarnow St.

"Is that what you wanted to show me, Lord? That, through all the years, You rooted Yourself in my soul so deep that nothing that ever happened in the long walk of my life could change that?"

I could feel tears starting to come, because standing on that corner reliving the steps of my life, I felt a calm yet riveting assurance and understanding of Psalm 23:6: *Surely goodness and mercy will follow me all the days of my life; and I will dwell in the house of the Lord forever.*[20]

Goodness and Mercy had certainly followed me all of my days. They had been my continued strength and blessing through every step. All the days—every one!

Beauty for Ashes

On this spot, God pulled back the shadow that had consumed me and let the beauty of the light that had always been there shine through. I felt a closeness to Him there unlike anything I had felt before.

He was cradling my heart.

Although God speaks to me at multiple locations in Detroit, we have already established "our" favourite spot. I meet Him there before leaving for home. I follow the same scenario each time.

---

20 NKJV.

I begin by driving through the Mexican business area, not only to be reminiscent of some of my dearest friends but because God has given me a real "heart-bond" with the Hispanic culture. I then work my way over and begin driving along 14th Street past my high school. I was so very blessed that a thoughtful friend surprised me last year with the opportunity to visit back inside the school. It is now being brought back from neglect and disarray, currently being used as business offices. I was thrilled to discover they were planning on keeping the inside intact, even so far as to leaving the lockers exactly as they were.

It makes me think about all of us. No matter what age we are, we should draw on the value and goodness that was originally placed inside us. It has great meaning, and someone else will benefit from what's in there.

Once I round the corner of the front of the building, I head towards the small alley-like laneway that runs along the back. This is where I can gauge the reconstruction that has transpired since my last visit. I drive down the lane past a small field that never materialized into the gym we would have all loved.

I can always feel the excitement and anticipation as I am nearing Dalzelle St. at the end of the laneway.

This is it! My special place with God.

Possibly, at this point you may think me slightly crazy. How can a city block riddled with debris, graffiti-ridden abandoned buildings, and homeless people possibly be that extra-special place God and I meet? Well, just as God is not a respecter of persons, He is also not a respecter of places. There is nowhere He doesn't occupy. The beauty is truly in the eye of the beholder.

> Just as God is not a respecter of persons, He is also not a respecter of places. There is nowhere He doesn't occupy.

There is generally only a handful of people around when I am there. Just like the scenario with the street I lived on, I initially stopped here out of curiosity about a building that is off the street across a grassy lot. The exterior totally intrigued me. It reminded me of an abstract piece of art.

Behind it looms the abandoned Roosevelt Hotel, the place I consumed copious amounts of the most delicious French fries and gravy ever known to mankind during my high school years.

The Dream House: Our special place.

Even though I refer to this location as "the place Detroit hugs me goodbye," it really is much more. This is the visual tool God used to help me understand His plan and take that first step into my new future. On this particular day, I knew I was going to be there for a while. God had much to show me.

I walked into the middle of the grassy lot and stared at the building. Both of us were obviously exposed to the area and the elements. At first glance, it was hard not to notice just how run down and damaged it was. Because I am so visually stimulated by colour, I was immediately drawn to the bright blue tarp held on by slats of wood in an attempt to keep the unwanted ravages of rain and snow out. I imagined most of the shingles being broken, damaged, or missing underneath. There were obvious signs of external "decorating" by either random artists—whose talents beautify the canvases comprised of the exteriors of less than desirable buildings—or the zealots of political statements.

> "Give me the plan, God! Don't I have the right to live a life of joy, purpose, and the fulfillment of my dreams?"

I began to wonder why God had prompted me to stop. Passersby may have expressed confusion as to what I was doing as I walked around that lot looking up and talking to the sky. "Give me the plan, God! Don't I have the right to live a life of joy, purpose, and the fulfillment of my dreams?"

It was spitting rain, and my mind went to Isaiah 55:10–11, *My word is like the snow and the rain that come down from the sky to water the earth… So also will be the word that I speak—it will not fail to do what I plan for it; it will do everything I send it to do.*[21]

"Then, speak to me, *please!*"

The Dream is Now

I started to turn slowly and look around the area. I realized that from the centre of this field I was able to turn in any direction and be looking towards a street that would lead me to many of the most significant events of my life. As I pivoted around towards the building, my eyes fixed on the wording on the roof.

"The dream is now." That was it! This is what God brought me here to tell me!

I had been waiting for Him to tell me what I needed to do to enter into the purpose that would be my life now along with the realization of my new desires and dreams. I was already there! I just had to take the first step. No planning, no controlling, no preconceived expectations—only the joy of taking the steps with Him. This was a very foreign concept for me, but so was the life I had found myself in after losing Michael. The design for my future would

---

21 GNT.

be new and it would be perfect, no matter what I came against.

In that moment, my mind moved to a place of thankfulness. Even though I lacked a tangible plan for my future, I began to concentrate on all the positive gifts God had instilled in me. These gifts and talents were not driven or measured by my quality as a wife but rather by my willingness to walk in what God had already planned from the moment He "formed" me. If He was pulling me forward, I had to give Him something to use.

I drove home that day, more than a year after God had first spoken to me, having no idea what I should be doing but confident that was exactly the perfect place to be.

chapter ten
Walking Me Home

After arriving home, I awoke the next morning in a panic. *Who are you kidding? You'll never do it! You're too much of a control freak! And what about the remaining elements of your grief?*

I sat upright and thought, *no*! God hadn't done all this talking for nothing. I was not about to let doubt and fear come in and slam the door that had just been opened. I was turning a corner and not stepping back.

Lesson from a Moving House

I whispered a short prayer: "You're going to have to help me, Lord." I grabbed my coffee and checked Facebook to see how my friends had weathered the previous day and night. I decided to post a photo pertaining to "turning the corner," in hopes that a public declaration would spur me on.

While searching through some images, I came across a picture and began to laugh. I couldn't help but think this was the perfect picture of what my life

> I was not about to let doubt and fear come in and slam the door that had just been opened.

would now be, and I felt strangely okay with that.

It showed a large building—or possibly a stately home—being moved on wheels. It was obviously turning a corner as people watched its every move, wondering where its final destination would be. Nothing about its appearance would indicate it was suffering any distress.

My life now.

This was me, all right. There was a time I had been securely planted in my home, living a life with no question of what my role or purpose was. My routine was perfect, and I had very little stress or concern. Now I was uprooted and rolling. And just as the passersby in this photo wondered about the final destination of the building, I had no idea where I was heading. But just as the wheels and equipment under this house knew the precise calibrations to cause it to roll into the place of perfection of purpose, I would allow God to do the same thing.

The most interesting part of the visual was the church and cross that became visible as the house turned the corner. This reminded me of who and what would be guiding me around every corner.

I had made a decision to embrace my life.

My grief will most likely still rear its ugly head in the most unexpected and unlikely places, and there is the possibility that there are pictures, objects, and places I may never be able to look at or visit because the pain is too gripping. But I am okay with that. I couldn't expect to suffer a loss as deep

> I couldn't expect to suffer a loss as deep and debilitating as I had without feeling the effects for possibly even a lifetime. Even so, I would not let it define me.

and debilitating as I had without feeling the effects for possibly even a lifetime. Even so, I would not let it define me.

I let go of the concepts that my relationship with my family was defined by being married to their father or that my grandchildren could only experience a certain type of relationship with me if they had both their grandparents intact. My perfect family had changed but my perfect love for them hadn't. I would now embrace my role with a new, fervent vigour.

I realized that even though there is nothing like being loved by a man who is totally devoted to you, I would survive without that if God called me to. Only He would be able to open my heart to that possibility. I take every ounce of love I feel from family and friends as a beautiful, comforting, life-giving gift, always cherished.

My Biggest Decision

My biggest decision was to live life much like that rolling house in the picture. I would not be reckless or fly by the seat of my pants; however, I would be open to my dreams and goals changing should the need or opportunity arise. If that were to happen, I would replace feelings of defeat or failure with anticipation of new adventures being led by God.

My days would now be filled with the wonder of what might be in store to surprise or delight me, and in times of uncertainty I would lean on those who truly loved and cared for me. I was not alone.

My Bucket List would now always end with "and…" leaving place for continued additions, for I was open to every adventure God had in store. I would believe in the fulfillment of the desires of my heart.

> I was open to every adventure God had in store.

More than ever, it became vitally clear that life is short and we are living in a broken world—not at all the world God had planned. There is great pain, loneliness, and despair. But alongside also runs an endless supply of love, compassion, caring, and concern. I knew I could no longer focus on a plan for my life but rather began focusing on offering enough love and compassion to those around me for whatever time God deemed fit for me to be here. That was "His" plan, and I would embrace it with all I had in me.

Walking Each Other Home

I once came across a statement that said, *When it comes right down to it, we are all just walking each other home.*

That one statement brought back memories of what it was like to be asked for the honour of allowing someone to escort me home. It conveyed several possible emotions on the part of the "ask-ee":

- They were interested in you, they had feelings that caused them to genuinely want to be in your presence.
- You held a place of worth that someone else might not.
- Love might even enter the equation.
- Physical touch was often an anticipated bonus.
- Conversations of admiration and encouragement would flow freely.
- It would demonstrate a level of genuine feelings.

- On occasion you felt protected, and there were times acts of service entered into what was needed to be done.
- But most importantly, they sought you out. You were important enough for them to take the risk, even though it might end in rejection.

I was now able to see the plan that four years before had been a seed planted in the depths of my pain. I can't control life and its circumstances or even remotely understand why things happen. I can't control the effects of the evil in this world or the amount of suffering we go through. But I can put my hands into the hands of the lives of those around me and ask if I can walk them home. I can let go of wanting to orchestrate what I feel my life should be, and instead, embrace what and whom God brings my way.

And in the end, if I walk with a heart that truly demonstrates Christ's love, I hope one day I will stand before God and He will point to the faces of those whose hands I held, whose lives I may have affected, and He will say, *I'm glad you remembered My address. Thanks for walking them home.*

chapter eleven

There is Freedom

A very famous monument in downtown Detroit is "The Spirit of Detroit." It's a large bronze statue of a seated man, a work of art that was dedicated to the city in 1958. In his left hand is a golden sphere emanating rays to symbolize God and in his right hand are figures of a family. The most interesting feature of the monument is the inscription on the wall behind it. It is from 2 Corinthians 3:17: *now the Lord is that spirit, and where the spirit of the Lord is, there is liberty.*

> When I came back to where God "lives," and embraced all aspects of His Spirit, I regained my liberty to live life to its fullest.

If I have realized anything in the past four years, it is the truth that lies in the words of that Scripture verse. When I came back to where God "lives," and embraced all aspects of His Spirit, I regained my liberty to live life to its fullest. But with all liberty and freedom comes responsibility.

I was in the middle of writing *How to Kiss Without Using Your Lips* when God stopped me to write this book, and trust me, it was last thing I had thought of doing. I had begun to feel my creative self-returning, and I had a specific message to convey in my new writing endeavour. I was not interested in revisiting my excruciating pain and much less intrigued at sharing it in a book.

God had very different plans.

The Spirit of Detroit

Reminders

Every morning after I shower, I glance at the variety of encouraging messages, Scripture verses, and focus reminders I have taped to my bathroom mirror. I concentrate on their individual value because God has used them to speak to, encourage, or motivate me.

There is a rainbow drawn by my Grandson Kale, which was given to me on a day when I was feeling weary. I was attempting to do some hefty "self-talk" about relying on God's promises when Kale approached me, picture in hand. With certainty in his voice, he said, "God wants me to tell you His promises are true." It is a beautiful reminder every day.

Kale's rainbow.

Another "Grandcasso" (a picture that is as valuable as a Picasso because it is created by my grandchildren) by Layla is from her younger days, but it was perfectly timed when I had doubts about "making it" on my own. She gave it to me after children's church, and it boldly states, Be strong and have courage; Do not be afraid (Joshua 1:9).

> I praise God, because He did not reject my prayer or keep back His constant love from me.

One sticky note has Psalm 66:16, 19, and 20 on it. *Come and listen, all who honor God, and I will tell you what he has done for me… God has indeed heard me; he has listened to my prayer. I praise God, because He did not reject my prayer or keep back His constant love from me.*[22] I read it aloud every morning, along with Jeremiah 29:11 and Isaiah 41:9–10, and then I generally sit down with my coffee and my devotional for that day.

On one particular morning I decided to forego my regular devotional and simply read my Bible. I went to Isaiah. It's one of my favourite books. For

---

22 GNT.

some reason, it always delivers both strength and comfort to me. This day I flipped through the pages and began reading Isaiah 61:1–4.

The Sovereign Lord has filled me
with his Spirit.
He has chosen me and sent me
To bring good news to the poor,
To heal the broken-hearted,
To announce release to captives
And freedom to those in prison.
He has sent me to proclaim
That the time has come
When the Lord will save his people
And defeat their enemies.
He has sent me to comfort all who mourn,
To give to those who mourn in Zion
Joy and gladness instead of grief,
A song of praise instead of sorrow.
They will be like trees
That the Lord himself has planted.
They will all do what is right,
And God will be praised for what he has done.
They will rebuild cities that have
long been in ruins.

God Rolled His Eyes and Cleared His Throat

I sat there staring at the words. I wouldn't allow my mind to think. I felt like a child enthralled in an activity, unwilling to raise their head because they knew their parent was standing directly in front of them, waiting to pose a question they didn't want to answer.

I could have sworn I heard God clear His throat to get my attention. I could no longer keep my thoughts frozen. I closed my eyes and heard, *well?*

> I could have sworn I heard God clear His throat to get my attention.

I tried to play stupid, "Well, what, Lord?"

If there is ever a time God rolls His eyes, He would have in that moment. I knew what was coming, and He knew that I knew. I just needed a nudge, a reminder. I could feel Him, but this wasn't one of those bask-in–the-glory-of-His-love-and-healing moments. He was going to push me into doing something I hadn't wanted to.

And then it came, that still small voice...

Mary Anne, each morning I watch you stand in front of that mirror saying, "Come and listen, all who honor God, and I will tell you what He has done for me." Exactly who are you telling?

I instantly had a rebuttal. "I'm saying it as praise to You and a reminder to myself of what you have brought me through."

You're not praising Me by keeping it to yourself. Write a book.

"Oh, no, no, no, Lord! Not that! Please don't ask me! It will be too painful to dredge up all those events. I am already in the middle of another book, and surely no one is interested in hearing about my pain. What if no one buys it, no one reads it?" I thought perhaps that question would somehow change His mind.

The Importance of One

Mary Anne, what if one person buys it, what if one person reads it, what if one person is comforted in the midst of debilitating pain and suffering? What if one person finds MY address in this book? You were that one person, and I came for you. Isn't that one person worth it?

I cried for a very long time. I was taken back to the feelings of my deepest despair and how I longed for comfort and relief from the gut wrenching pain. I was oblivious to anyone around me and what they were going through during that time—I wanted someone to come for me. It was then I felt a sense of responsibility. How could I not reach out to that one, no matter what it took?

It is my deepest desire that, if you are reading these words, you realize you are that one. If you have been in that "forsaken zone," have suffered the loss of a loved one, the loss of a marriage or the dream for what you thought your life would be, there is a place where God is waiting for you, wanting to give you strength. If you had forgotten where it was, I hope as you turned from page to page you felt my hand slip into yours and I was able to… walk you home.

> There is a place where God is waiting for you

If you have never been there, close your eyes, and ask God where it is. He'll point you in exactly the right direction. And just as He was with me, He will be the same with you—standing at the front door, arms wide open, just waiting … for the one.

About the Author

Mary Anne K. Moran was born in Windsor, Ontario, Canada, to an Irish father and Italian mother. Although her birth took place in Canada, she was raised in Detroit, Michigan from infanthood until her late teens, when as a result of her father's dependence on kidney dialysis, a decision was made to move to Ontario.

From an early age her love of writing and speaking was evident. She was always the first to volunteer to step to the front of the class for speeches, and anxiously waited for any assignment requiring story writing or essays. Those who know her will attest to the fact that her "gift of the gab" flows freely when given the opportunity to let it go.

Professionally, her experience in the natural health industry spans more than two and a half decades. She has held executive sales, management, and educational positions with such companies as GNC and Beverly Hills Weight Loss Clinics. She has also served as Canadian Director of Education and Communication for Garden of Life Inc. Her experience in lecturing, teaching, and ministry, spans across the USA, Canada, and Central America.

Personally, Mary Anne resides in Barrie, Ontario, Canada. She is the mother of three grown married daughters, and is perfecting her spoiling techniques on her five perfect grandchildren.

In 2011 Mary Anne suffered the tragic and unexpected loss of her husband Michael after nearly 30 years of marriage.

In 2014, after surfacing from a journey through intense grief and re-inventing herself, Mary Anne realized life was not meant to merely "survive" but to "thrive". She began writing again, and seeking new venues for speaking and influencing the people placed before her. Her warm personality, sense of humour, practical approach to life, along with her uninhibited, spontaneous displays of love towards even the remotest stranger, makes her a very sought after speaker.

Mary Anne has every intent of fulfilling the following quote:

"When I stand before God at the end of my life, I would hope that I would not have a single bit of talent left, and could say…. I used everything You gave me!" —*Erma Bombeck*[23]

---

23 "Erma Bombeck Quotes." *Brainyquote*. 22 February, 2016 (http://www.brainyquote.com/quotes/authors/e/erma_bombeck.html).

M.A.K. (Mary Anne) Moran
Author/Keynote Speaker

For information regarding speaking
engagements or book orders, please contact:

Mary Anne K. Moran
Office: 705 726-2286
Toll-Free Office 866 244-1118 (Canada & USA)
or info@makmoran.com

Website: makmoran.com
Facebook: MAK MORAN
Twitter: @makmoran
Instagram: makm55
LinkedIn: Mary Anne K. Moran
(Author/International Keynote Speaker)

Also by M.A.K. Moran

Before I Knew You Loved Me
1-897373-42-2

The first time my cousin asked me why my mother liked my sister more than me, I felt a real sense of being exposed. The realization that the roles of division that dictated our in-house behaviour were not carefully hidden, as I had thought, but were, in fact, visible to the outside world created a mindset that kept me feeling less than adequate compared to those around me. Never once did it occur to me to ask for help or even be aware I needed it...

"Before I Knew You Loved Me is a transparent and moving story of one woman's search for acceptance, personal identity, and love. It will get you thinking about the health of your own family relationships."

—Glen R. Pitts
Former Director
Cities of the World/Campus Crusade for Christ